Sue Leather

Series Editor: Rob Waring
Story Editor: Julian Thomlinson
Series Development Editor: Sue Leather

HEINLE

Australia • Bra.   • United States

HEINLE
CENGAGE Learning·

Page Turners Reading Library

Light
Sue Leather

Publisher: Andrew Robinson

Executive Editor: Sean Bermingham

Senior Development Editor:
Derek Mackrell

Assistant Editor: Sarah Tan

Director of Global Marketing:
Ian Martin

Content Project Manager:
Tan Jin Hock

Print Buyer:
Susan Spencer

Layout Design and Illustrations:
Redbean Design Pte Ltd

Cover Illustration: Eric Foenander

Photo Credits:
79 (top) Bryan Busori/Shutterstock,
(bottom) Thomas Barrat/Shutterstock,
80 (top) miralex/iStockphoto,
(bottom) timurka/iStockphoto,
81 Andrew Horne/Wikimedia Commons,
82 Marins Arnesen/Wikimedia Commons,
83 (top) Baumi/Wikimedia Commons,
(bottom) Luigi Guarino/Flickr

ISBN-13: 978-1-4240-4664-5

ISBN-10: 1-4240-4664-5

Heinle
20 Channel Center Street
Boston, Massachusetts 02210
USA

Cengage Learning is a leading provider of customized learning solutions with office locations around the globe, including Singapore, the United Kingdom, Australia, Mexico, Brazil, and Japan. Locate your local office at:
international.cengage.com/region

Cengage Learning products are represented in Canada by Nelson Education, Ltd.

Visit Heinle online at **elt.heinle.com**

Visit our corporate website at
www.cengage.com

Printed in the United States of America
1 2 3 4 5 6 7 – 14 13 12 11 10

Contents

People in the story

Zelim Malin
leader of the Banda, a
political group now in
power in Kalastia

Jago
Gora's friend and a member
of the resistance

Kotya
a young soldier in the
Kalastian army

Amir Kalev
Arda's father

The story is set in Kalastia, an imaginary country.

Chapter 1

The beginning

"What do you mean, destroyed?"

Arda Kalev sat up in her bed suddenly. A few moments ago she had been fast asleep. Now she was listening to Timur Datka, the Head Librarian from the National Library, on the telephone as he told her that her sculpture *Together* had been broken into thousands of pieces.

"But who . . . ?"

The librarian told her that it was the Banda military police. "I couldn't do anything, Ms. Kalev," he said, obviously sad. "They just came in and destroyed . . . well . . . almost everything."

Arda felt a lack of feeling come over her body, like she'd taken a painkiller.

Datka was going on, angry now, his voice rising. "'Un-Kalastian' they called it," he said. "They're . . . well . . . I don't know what to say. I'm so sorry."

Arda fell back onto her bed. Datka was still talking, but she couldn't listen to him anymore. In her head was the scene of the Banda military police in their ugly brown uniforms, taking a hammer to her sculpture. Her beautiful sculpture. She imagined the thousands of pieces of stone lying on the floor of the library entrance hall. She remembered the many months of work, the love that she had put into her creation. She remembered the feel of the stone as she shaped it. She remembered the day she had finally finished it and how she had felt as she looked at it. Something had been torn from her and it was painful. She felt a tight feeling that rose from her stomach into her throat, and then, suddenly, she

⋯ ⋯ ⋯ sounded around the room for a

long dark hall. Still, ⋯

happening. This was the first time the Banda had ⋯ ⋯ her work. Something was changing.

Arda picked up her jacket and walked into her studio, the place where she worked. The large room led out of the house and onto the street. It was beautifully quiet in the studio. She stopped for a moment and felt its stillness, felt the peace of its cool white walls. She listened to the silence. She thought how lovely it would be to stay there, to just . . . work. She looked at the large piece of white stone that was waiting for her. Then she took a deep breath and went through the door that led to Republic Street. Outside, the winter morning air was icy cold. She walked to Zuzu's Café on the corner.

Zuzu's was a café where artists like herself often went for coffee and conversation. These days it was nothing like it used to be before the Banda came to power, but still it was a place where people talked. Arda ordered coffee and began talking to a group of young artists. All the talk was of changes in the Banda. "They say that their new leader, Zelim Malin, is determined to destroy everything," Leyla Goruv, the young painter, said. There was talk that the liberal Jurka political party, some of whom were outside

Kalastia, were getting ready to fight for their country. Malin and the Banda were already at war, filling people with fear, destroying their enemies from within.

"Th[illegible] the National Gallery will be next," said Leyla [illegible] have a sculp[illegible] "Un-Kalastian" and destroyed, then why not *Light*?

Arda jumped up suddenly, leaving half a cup of coffee on the table.

"Where are you going?" asked Leyla Gurov.

But Arda had already gone.

Chapter 2

The National Gallery

Arda ran down the street toward the National Gallery, past the men putting up huge pictures of Zelim Malin around Republic Square.

The door of the National Gallery was closed and the notice outside said "Closed for cleaning." Arda took out her cell phone and rang Gora Bey's number.

"Arda!" he said. "Come round to the back door. I'll be there in two or three minutes."

Arda walked round to the back of the National Gallery building and stood at the small blue door. A moment later, it opened. A small, gray-haired man with round glasses appeared.

"It's good to see you, Arda," Gora Bey said, standing back to look at her. "You look more like your mother every day." Bey was the curator at the National Gallery. He had been a friend of Yana, Arda's mother, when they were both at university and then through her career in politics. They had been close right up until her death eight years before, and he had always been a frequent visitor at the Kalev home. Arda had known him since she was a little girl.

Arda smiled at Bey, but she couldn't hide her worry from him.

"There's something wrong, isn't there?" said Bey, as they walked up the stairs and into the gallery. "What is it?" He stopped and turned toward her, his kind eyes looking into hers.

8

Arda told him about *Together*. Her words came out quickly, and she tried not to cry.

Gora Bey slowly shook his head. "Even *you*?" he said. "Things are worse than I thought."

"Th~~ey said it was un~~-Kalastian," said Arda. "And now . . ."

"Our country's greatest art is here, Arda," Gora Bey said, he waved his hands towards the walls. "Wonderful, isn't it?"

Arda was hardly listening to the old man. She looked anxiously for her sculpture.

"Zelim Malin is very dangerous," Bey went on. "They say he had Lazev killed."

Lazev had been the previous Banda leader. He was bad enough, but Zelim Malin was worse.

"And he hates us, Arda," Bey told her. "All thinkers, writers, artists."

Where was it? They must be getting to the end of the gallery soon. Arda walked faster.

"All these paintings are in danger now that he has taken over as the leader," Bey said, almost running to keep close to Arda. "I've closed the Gallery for a few days, but I can't close it forever . . ."

They had finally reached the end of the main gallery. Arda breathed out loud. There it was at last! Her statue, *Light*. It was a statue of a young woman in white stone cut from the mountains of Kalastia. The young woman was looking into

the distance. Art experts had said that she seemed to be looking outside Kalastia to the world. The statue was beautiful in the natural light from the window just above it.

Arda breathed out loud again. "I have to take it, Gora," she said. "I have to take it now, to put it somewhere safe!"

Arda turned to look at the old family friend.

"It's not just your work," he said to her. He was quieter now, but serious. "Things have changed, Arda. Now under this Zelim Malin, the Banda seem to be destroying all real works of art. They've already started . . ."

"But what can I do about that?"

"I don't know," said Bey. He bit his lip as he always did when he was thinking. Then he said, "But you can't just take *Light* and not think about the other works of art."

Arda's voice got louder. "I'm just an artist, Gora," she said. "I'm not a politician."

Bey didn't mention her mother, but Arda could feel her name, unspoken, in the air. "What can any of us do?" he said.

Now that Arda really looked at the old man, she could see how worried he looked. "What about the Jurka?" she asked. Leyla Bey had told her that the Jurka political party was organizing, getting ready to fight. She knew that Gora Bey was a Jurka follower. After all, he had been a close friend of her mother's.

"Agh!" said Gora Bey, throwing up his arms. "The Jurka. It's true that they—we—are organizing. But things are different now. There are no real leaders . . ."

Arda looked carefully at the old man. It was dangerous to admit that you were a member of the Jurka party these days. "I'll send someone to collect *Light*," she said, turning to go.

"They miss your mother," the old man said.

Arda didn't answer, but ran downstairs and into the street. Once outside, she breathed deeply. She went quickly towards home. She had to get back to the quiet of her studio.

I just want to work, she thought.

Chapter 3

A walk through Galata

she do? It wasn't jus...
she save *Light*, and let the Banda destroy the rest. The
entire national art collection! If Gora was right, they would
destroy everything. Arda put the phone down.

She tried to work instead. She looked into the corner of the
room at the large piece of new white stone that she had
ordered to work on. She had thought that she would start a
new piece of work, but she still hadn't decided what it
would be. She stared at it, looking for the shape that it
would become. The time just before starting a new work
was usually one of her favorite times. She often spent hours
looking at the stone, waiting for a shape to come into her
head, waiting for an idea. This act of creation was a special
time for her. But now, her head was full of other thoughts
and she just couldn't work.

Arda went to bed, hoping that she would feel better the
next day. But she didn't. The next morning she still couldn't
work, and she still didn't know what to do about *Light*.

I have to get some air, Arda thought. She put on her jacket
and went outside into the cold morning air. She walked
through the backstreets of Galata, her mind lost in thought.

As an artist, she had to save her own work for the future, she said to herself. That was her duty. As for the rest of it, what could she do? *I'm not a politician,* she thought. *I just want to work.*

"T... ...1"

his head. She watched

lying on the ground next to the man, its pages torn.

Arda jumped into the door of a building so that she could not be seen.

"This is a dirty, foreign un-Kalastian book," shouted the policeman.

She heard the man crying for help. They were beating him for reading a foreign novel! They were beating a man for reading a book, and only she was there to see it. What could she do? "Sooner or later, Arda," her mother used to say, "you have to stand up and fight." But if she tried to help the man, no doubt they would beat her, too! She came out of the door of the building and walked quickly away from the café, toward National Avenue. Her heart was beating loudly and she felt the fear on her body. She didn't look back.

This was the first time she'd been to National Avenue for about two weeks. Now it was lined with pictures of Zelim Malin. The image of his large handsome face and black hair was everywhere. It was posted on buildings and even on

BEWARE OF
ENEMIES TO
KALASTIA!

the trees on either side of the street. He wore the brown
uniform of the Banda. They called him *The Great General*.
"May The Great General rule us for a thousand years!" it
said under the pictures. There were huge new posters along
the street too, with writing on them. "Kalastians!" screamed

Then, as she approached even closer, she saw that they were
throwing books onto the fire! They were burning books
from the library. "Un-Kalastian rubbish!" one of them
shouted as he threw a thick book onto the fire.

Arda walked past a large number of books, just lying on
the street. She walked quickly but tried to look at them, to
read their covers. It was a great mountain of books by
writers both living and dead. Shakespeare was there,
Goethe, Balzac, Dante, Austen, Tolstoy, Murasaki Shikibu.
All the great foreign writers were here. But there were
Kalastian writers, too—Kalastian writers who were
supposed to be "un-Kalastian" for some reason, she
guessed: Borov, Safin, Bekturova. The Banda were burning
books by the greatest writers in the world!

"What do you want?" shouted one of the policemen, a
young man no older than she was. He looked toward her
angrily. His eyes were like the eyes of an animal, thought
Arda. "What are you staring at?" he asked. He moved, as if
to walk toward her. As he moved, she saw that he moved
his hand toward his gun. "Do you want to burn some
books yourself?" he said.

"No, I . . ." she said, her voice weak. She looked away and walked on.

"Come on!" the policeman shouted after her. "Come and get yourself warm!" Arda hurried on. What could she do? What was happening? Somewhere in the distance she could hear the sound of gunshots.

As she walked on, Arda found that tears were rolling down her face. She lifted a hand to wipe them away. She was frightened by the violence that she had seen. But it was more than just fear. It was anger. What was happening to her city, to her country? They were changing the names of the streets, beating people for reading foreign writers, destroying works of art, burning books. Nothing was safe. Nobody was safe.

She had turned away from the police beating the young man, from the police burning the books, but how long could she go on turning away? Arda remembered her mother. "You have to fight for what you believe in," she had always said to her. Jana Kalev had always fought for what she believed in. A natural leader, she found it easy to live her life in public as a Jurka politician. *It was easy for her*, thought Arda, *but what can I do? I'm not brave like her.*

She thought about Gora. She saw the worry on his face. She thought about the art of the Kalastian national collection— all the paintings, the sculptures, everything. It was all at risk, all in danger. "Un-Kalastian!" she said out loud as she walked. How could art made in Kalastia be un-Kalastian? What was Kalastian, according to Zelim Malin?

She had to do something! She had to go back to the National Gallery. She had an idea and she had to talk to Gora Bey about it.

Chapter 4

Arda's idea

"Now slow ~~down~~,
I've just made some tea." Bey gave Arda ~~a cup~~
with plants from the mountains around Galata.

A few moments later, Arda explained her idea. "My father has all this art somewhere—art that belonged to my grandparents. It isn't very good. In fact, it's really bad. He only keeps it because it belonged to his parents. But it has subjects from Kalastian history, and has some historical value. It will keep the Banda happy, I think."

"I don't understand . . ."

"Well, what if we bring the pieces of art that my father has," Arda explained, "and put them in the Gallery?"

She took a drink of her tea. "Then we can take away all the real art from the Gallery and hide it somewhere," she went on. "That way, if the Banda military police come . . ."

"They'll find the worthless art!" finished Gora.

They were both quiet for a moment.

Then Gora asked, "But what about the people who come to visit the National Gallery? I'll have to re-open it soon."

"We can say that it's a new display," said Arda. "Anyway, everyone is so frightened at the moment, no one will say anything."

"Mmm . . . perhaps," said Gora.

"We have to try, Gora!" Arda said. "We have no choice."

"That's true," said Gora. "There's doesn't seem to be another way."

"The only thing I don't know," Arda went on, "is where to hide the real art, or how to get it out of the building without anyone seeing it."

Gora looked at Arda and bit his lip. There was silence for a moment as both of them thought.

Suddenly Gora said, "Mmm, I wonder . . ."

"What?"

"Maybe there's a way," he said. "Come with me."

Arda looked at him. She wondered what the "way" was.

"Follow me," said the old man. "I have something to show you." He smiled, pleased with himself.

Arda got up and followed Gora to the far end of the gallery. The old man walked quickly. He stopped next to an extremely old Kalastian wall hanging, a kind of carpet on the wall. It showed a picture of a hunter on his horse. The hunter had a large bird on his arm. Gora looked at the wall hanging, looked at Arda, and smiled.

"Well?" asked Arda. "What's this?"

The old man's eyes shone. "Look," he said. As he spoke, he lifted the wall hanging. Behind it was a space, and inside it was a handle made of metal. Gora pulled the handle down

and Arda heard a loud noise somewhere behind her. She turned round to see the wooden wall behind her opening.

Arda jumped. "What's that?" she asked.

"Come!" said Gora.

They walked over to the wooden wall. "See!" said Gora.

Arda looked, and where the wooden wall had moved, she saw some stone stairs. They went down below the building. "What's that?" she asked.

"Stairs!" said Gora, laughing. "They go down into a tunnel. A very long tunnel. It hasn't been used for many, many years . . . and nobody knows about it except me."

"A tunnel?" asked Arda. "Where does it lead?"

"To an old church just outside the city," Gora replied. "There are quite a lot of tunnels under Galata. They were made hundreds of years ago during the wars between the different churches. A lot of them had secret doors, so that people could escape easily. "

Arda looked at the old man. She knew that he was very knowledgeable about art. She realized he probably also knew more about the history of the capital city than anyone.

"The tunnel isn't used any more, of course . . . and it's dirty," Gora went on. "It could be dangerous, but perhaps . . ."

Arda suddenly started to laugh.

"What . . . ?"

"Gora, you're wonderful!" she said, kissing the old man on his head. "Now, who can help us?"

Chapter 5

"But they ɪᴇ ᴄᴄ
"Absolutely terrible! I caɪɪᴄ ᴄ
nationalistic rubbish! That's why they ɪᴄ ᴄ
the basement. They're worthless." Ever since Arda wᴜᴄ
child, the family had used the large basement room under
the house to put things they didn't use: old chairs and
tables, unwanted clothes. Now the basement was full of
stuff, and since Arda's mother had died, nothing was ever
thrown away.

"But that's exactly the point, Father," said Arda. "We need
something worthless for the Gallery."

"Well, fine," said Amir Kalev. "Come and get the paintings
anytime you like."

Arda arranged to collect the art that night. They had to act
quickly. In the meantime, Gora Bey had called in one of
the National Gallery workers, and the young man had
now arrived.

"Arda, this is Jago," Gora Bey said. "He works here at the
National Gallery, and I've known him since he was a child."
Jago was a tall, strong-looking man in his late twenties. He
had brown wavy hair and an open, pleasant face. Arda
liked him immediately.

Arda explained the plan to him. "We'll need more people," she said, "people we can trust."

"I can bring Ivo and Nazar," said Jago. "They sometimes help us to move art and I know we can trust them. Then we can arrange for more people to help us at the church. Leave it to me."

Two hours later it was dark. Arda, Jago, and the two other young men got into Jago's truck and drove to Amir Kalev's large house just outside the city.

"Hello, father," said Arda, as she kissed the top of the old man's head in the Kalastian sign of respect. She introduced the group to him in his comfortable living room.

"Good evening, sir," said Jago to Amir Kalev. "It's wonderful to meet you, and to be working with other followers of the Jurka." It was the first time that he had mentioned it, but Arda had guessed that Jago was a follower of the Jurka.

Amir Kalev was now in his seventies and a retired lawyer. Though he had never been in public life as his wife had, he had been a famous member of the Jurka in his day. "These are dangerous times to be in the Jurka," the older man said seriously. "You should all be very careful." He looked at the young men and then finally at his daughter. Amir didn't say anything to her, but Arda knew that he was thinking about Jana Kalev, the wife whom he had lost eight years before.

"Come on," said Arda, "we don't have much time."

Quickly, the four of them took the paintings from the basement of the Amir Kalev's house and loaded them into Jago's truck. Then Jago drove them to the old church. On the way he called the other young people who would help

them. When Arda, Jago, Ivo, and Nazar arrived at the old
ь **-rh**, they were met by five more people—three young
-ng women—all dressed in dark clothes.
" **said** Jago, smiling. "Lovers
-olitical party."

auvᴇⅈⅈ

Arda smiled at ɹₐgₒ
helping," she said to them.

"You're welcome," said one of the young women, **ѕⅈⅈ..**
"When Jago told us your idea, there was no way we could
say no."

"We have to resist these Banda thugs!" said one of the
young men.

"Come on." Arda led them inside the church. Gora had told
her exactly where the tunnel came out.

Well inside the dark church, Arda lifted a stone square and
showed the others the door in the floor that led to the
tunnel. "You see?" she said. "If you go down these stone
steps, you'll get to the tunnel that leads all the way to the
National Gallery."

"How long is the tunnel?" asked one of the young men.

"Gora said it's about a kilometer," said Arda.

"Let's work quickly, friends," said Jago. "We have just six or
seven hours before it starts to get light again."

And we have a lot to do, thought Arda. She wondered if they
would manage it. They had to get the worthless art into the
National Gallery, then hide the real art in the tunnel. Would

there be enough time? If it got light and the Banda saw them, they would be in real danger. The picture of the Banda police beating the student came into her mind. She ~~~~ her head to try to remove the memory.

~~~~ ~~~~ into the

were we~ ~ they had gotten all the paintings ~~ ~~~ leading into the National Gallery.

Arda looked at the others. They looked cold and very tired. She went up the stairs and knocked on the secret door. There was silence. She knocked again, louder this time. *Come on, Gora*, she thought. There was another silence, which seemed to go on forever. Then she heard a noise inside the Gallery. Suddenly, the secret door opened and Gora's smiling face appeared. "There you are!" he said.

The old man showed them where to put Arda's grandparents' art. They worked quickly, moving the worthless pieces up the stairs and into the gallery. After they had finished, Gora gave them some strong coffee, which they drank quickly.

"OK," said Arda, once they were all feeling a little better from the coffee. "Now all we have to do is to move all the real art into the tunnel!" She added with a smile, "And this time, be really careful, please. These pieces of art are not worthless at all."

Four hours later, every painting and every sculpture from the Kalastia National Gallery was inside the secret tunnel and covered carefully with sheets of plastic. The large statues were the most difficult to move. Finally, as the sun was rising, Gora and Arda started to hang the paintings they had brought from Amir Kalev's house on the walls of the National Gallery.

"Bye!" said Jago to Arda, as he turned to go. "And well done! It was all your plan. If you need my help again, just call me."

Jago gave Arda his card with his address and telephone number. Arda smiled and thanked Jago and his team of workers, but she knew that this was only the beginning. Gora now had to re-open the National Gallery.

"I'll stay here with you. We can say that I work here, too," said Arda to Gora. "It's only a matter of time before we have a visit from the Banda military police."

Chapter 6

...

Major Rakov ...
large black mustache. His neat ...
man of great energy, but no imagination. "Man ...
That's me," he always said to his men. He liked to tell them
that he had never read a book. He was the kind of man that
Zelim Malin really valued.

"You know," he said to Gora and Arda, "that our Great
General has said that all un-Kalastian works must
be destroyed."

Arda and Gora nodded.

"If I find anything un-Kalastian," the major continued in an
icy voice, "both of you will go to prison." He looked at
them carefully.

Arda's skin felt cold, the fear moving over her body. She
looked ahead, trying not to look into the eyes of Major
Rakov. *Will he be able to see how frightened I am?* she
wondered. She and Gora followed the police as they walked
down the main gallery.

"Mmm," he said, looking at a painting which showed a
battle scene from Kalastian history. "The Battle of Mendel.
A famous win for our great nation. Very good."

"Er . . . yes," said Gora.

"Well," said Major Rakov, "I don't know what you think, boys, but I think this is OK so far."

Arda looked at the young policemen. They all nodded their heads in agreement. She took a second look at one of them. He was a tall young man with very white skin. He looked familiar somehow, she thought. Where had she seen him before? She couldn't quite remember who he was, but she was certain that she knew him. He just stared ahead, not looking at her.

The huge black leather boots of the Banda made a heavy sound on the old wooden floor of the gallery as they walked. Slowly, they passed by the paintings that Arda had brought from her father's house. One by one, Rakov looked at the paintings. He seemed to approve of them all.

Finally they arrived at the old Kalastian wall hanging which hid the handle that opened the secret tunnel. Rakov and his men stopped and looked at it. Arda and Gora looked down. Arda held her breath. Would Rakov find the handle? Would he find the secret tunnel? Rakov and his men seemed to look at the hunting scene for a long time. Rakov touched his mustache. He went up to the wall hanging and held out his hand as if to touch it.

"What do you think of this painting, Major Rakov?" asked Arda suddenly.

Rakov turned round. Arda was pointing over to the other side of the gallery, where there was a large painting of a Kalastian leader from the nineteenth century. Major Rakov left the wall hanging and walked over to it. His men followed him.

"Mmm. Very . . . suitable," Rakov said.

Suitable thought Arda. *What a word to describe art!* But at least Rakov had forgotten about the wall hanging. The danger was past and soon the group of men were on their way to the door. Arda tried not to show her relief.

The tall young policeman and Arda walked behind Rakov. She looked at him again and suddenly remembered who he was. Kotya, his name was, or something like that. He had studied at Kalastia National Art School, where she too had studied. He was a year or two younger than she was, and they hadn't known each other that well. But it was him, of that she was certain.

Kotya turned towards Arda. "It's OK," he said, moving his lips without making a sound.

They were at the door, and Arda didn't have time to ask him anything.

"This all seems to be in order," said Major Rakov, his hand on the door. "For now," he added, looking at Arda and Gora with icy gray eyes.

As the door closed behind the Banda, Gora smiled at Arda.

"Well done!" he said. "They don't have any idea what's going on."

Arda smiled too, but she was still thinking about the young policeman.

Chapter 7

Danger

recog
about art. He must know.
National Gallery now wasn't the real matter
must know that it was just rubbish! What did he mean
when he said, "It's OK"? She couldn't take any chances.
Maybe Kotya had said something to Rakov. She had to go
to the National Gallery.

Arda got dressed. Gora always went to the Gallery very
early, around seven. She was restless. She walked up and
down her studio, waiting for the daylight. She looked at the
white stone for a while, but still nothing came to her. As
soon as it was light, she went to the National Gallery to
warn Gora.

They talked and had coffee. Then they waited. An hour
after arriving at the National Gallery, Arda looked through
the window. "It's Rakov!" she said to Gora. Major Rakov
was jumping out of his police van with his three men. One
of them was Kotya. They were followed by another van
with five other policemen. This time they didn't knock, but
kicked the door. Gora ran downstairs.

"Where is it?" shouted Rakov, as they walked into
the building.

"Wha . . . I . . ." Gora almost ran next to Rakov, as the Banda officer took huge steps up the stairs and into the gallery.

"Where IS it?" Rakov repeated, turning on the old man.

"I don't know wh . . ." Rakov lifted his hand and hit the old man so hard that he fell to the ground.

Arda quickly stepped in front of Gora so that Rakov couldn't hit him again. "I'm sorry," she said. "Mr. Bey . . ."

"Don't think that I'm stupid!" Rakov shouted, as he looked at Arda.

"I . . . uh . . . no." Arda spoke quietly.

"I think there is some un-Kalastian art here," Rakov went on. "I tell you, I intend to look everywhere for it. Everywhere!" He was already kicking tables and chairs and taking paintings off the walls.

Arda looked at Kotya. Had he told Rakov that there was more art? Kotya shook his head. "It wasn't me," he said to her silently. The young man looked unhappy, but before she had a chance to say anything to him, Rakov screamed, "Take both of them to prison!"

Two of the men came forward and took hold of Arda and Gora. The old man was shaking. The policemen dragged them away, and Rakov shouted, "I warn you—if we find any un-Kalastian art here, you will both be shot." One of the policeman put handcuffs on Arda and Gora so that they couldn't move their hands.

◇◇◇

As they were being thrown into the back of one of the vans, Arda heard Rakov shout the order to close the door of the

National Gallery and search everywhere. "And I mean everywhere!!" he screamed.

~~ ~~lice van drove off quickly. Arda and Gora were in ~~ ~~ front. Arda looked at Gora, ~~ ~~red

going to find ~~ ~~
she do? The van had no windows; she ~~ ~~
where they were exactly. But it was going very fast, and once she was at the police prison, she couldn't possibly escape.

Suddenly the van stopped. *They must be at a traffic light,* she thought. She looked at the door of the van. The traffic light must be red, but it wouldn't be red for long. Was it possible to open the handle with her handcuffed hands? It wouldn't be easy, but maybe . . . ? She looked at Gora, who had his eyes open. He too was looking at the door and looking at her. "Go!" he said to her, just moving his lips. "Go! Go!"

Arda leaned toward the door handle and pushed. Nothing happened. "Come on!" she said silently. She pushed again. To her surprise, the door suddenly opened, just as the van moved forward. The traffic light had changed to green! Unable to stop her fall with her hands, Arda fell heavily, her head hitting the ground. It hurt badly, but Arda got to her feet immediately and started running back the way they had driven. She turned around and saw that one of the policemen was running fast after her.

It was around eight-fifteen in the morning, and people were going through the city streets to work, either by car or on foot. Arda ran through the traffic and the people. She ran ⸺ she had ever run. She wasn't used to ⸺ her legs hurt and it

behind her.

Jago. I have to get to Jago's apartment, she ⸺ But where was it? He had given her his address card, but it was in her jacket pocket. Her hands were in handcuffs, so there was no way to look. She tried to remember the address. She knew it was Montag Street, but the number? She thought hard, trying to see the card and the number in her mind. Number 33? No, 35, she thought. Montag Street was just two or three streets away from here, in an area of the city called Sava. Breathless, she ran down a side street and through to Sava. As she turned down the street she looked back and saw the policeman still behind her.

Arda ran down Montag Street, a long street of gray apartment buildings. She looked at the first number. 201! Number 35 must be right down the other end of the street. She ran, hoping that the policeman was far enough behind that he couldn't catch her. She ran through the people walking to work. Where was number 35? She ran through the hundreds. Then it was number 99. She felt the blood from the cut on her head. It was flowing down her face. She saw the sixties, fifties, forties, flying past as she ran. She felt the taste of the blood in her mouth. She ran through the people, pushing, avoiding them. Finally there it was. Number 35. It was a tall apartment building with an open door. She hoped she'd got the number right.

She looked round. The policeman wasn't right behind her—he was running through the people too—so she jumped through the door and stood just inside. She put her head down. She took big breaths and tried to control her breathing. Now that she had stopped, she could feel a lot of pain from her face and head, and the blood was all over her jacket. She had to hide quickly!

Just then a young woman came down the stairs.

Arda had to take a chance. "Can you help me?" she asked quietly.

The young woman looked at Arda and at her head.

"It's important," said Arda, quickly. "Really important." Then she added, "I don't have time to explain, but I haven't done anything wrong."

The young woman looked Arda in the eyes.

"Please," said Arda.

"OK."

"There's a policeman following me," explained Arda. "Can you go outside and tell him that I've run down the street?"

The young woman walked out of the apartment block and waited for the policeman to arrive.

"Where is she?" the policeman shouted.

Arda held her breath.

"She went that way," she said, pointing down the street.

Arda waited and then watched as the Banda policeman ran past the door of the apartment building and down the street.

Chapter 8

A plan

Arda waited until she saw the Banda policeman disappear round the corner at the end of the street. She walked up to the lines of postboxes in the hall of the apartment building and looked for Jago's name. The building had sixteen floors, and there were a lot of postboxes. Finally she found the name Jago Dudin and the apartment number 914. That must be him! She took the lift up to the ninth floor.

Arda kicked against Jago's door. There was no answer. He wasn't home, she thought, and her cell phone was in the inside pocket of her jacket. With the handcuffs on, she couldn't get it without someone's help. What could she do? She looked at her watch. Eight thirty-five. It was already over thirty minutes since she and Gora had been taken from the National Gallery! In thirty minutes, Rakov and his men could easily find . . . She didn't want to think about it. She kicked again, but still there was no reply. She took the lift down to the street again. She tried to think clearly. She had to get Jago's cell number, and she had to phone him. She would have to get someone to help her, perhaps someone in a shop on the street.

Arda stood just inside the door and looked out onto the street. She looked right and left. The Banda policeman was nowhere to be seen. She started across the road toward a little shop.

"Arda!!"

She turned round. It was Jago! They both went quickly into the building.

"Jago!" she said. "Thank goodness!"

"What happened?" he asked.

On the way back upstairs in the lift, Arda told him quickly

her face and head with ....

"We have to get into the National Gallery," Arda said. We have to stop them finding the secret door."

"That's better," said Jago, looking at her head and putting something on the cuts.

"I have an idea," she went on. "We just need two cell phones, lights, some wire cutters . . . Oh, and Nazar and Ivo, too!"

◇◇◇

After Arda had explained the plan, Jago phoned his brother who owned a building company two streets away. "We need wire cutters," he explained to Arda. Then he picked up his cell phone. "Have you got your cell phone?" he asked.

"It's in my pocket," Arda said.

"OK, good," Jago said. "Now we have to cover you up a bit. He took a scarf and tied up Arda's hair, then they went downstairs. Jago looked out onto the street to make sure that the policeman hadn't come back. "OK," he said to Arda. "Get into the back of the truck." Arda got in and Jago covered her with a blue plastic sheet. Then he drove round to his brother's workshop and parked his truck inside the yard.

Jago's brother Ruslan was like an older Jago, with the same open smile and wavy brown hair. He acted like he saw a handcuffed woman in his workshop every day. He looked at her and at the handcuffs. "I have just the thing," he said. He took out a small, thin piece of metal and put it inside the lock of the handcuffs. He moved it a little, and before long the lock opened. It obviously wasn't the first time that Ruslan had opened handcuffs this way.

"Thank you!" said Arda.

"You're welcome," Ruslan said with a smile. "Now, the wire cutters."

Arda and Jago took the wire cutters from Ruslan, then drove off to pick up Ivo and Nazar. They all drove toward the old church just outside the city. "There are going to be military police everywhere," said Jago, "so I'm going to take a back road."

"Be careful," said Arda.

"Leave it to me," said Jago. He smiled his broad smile.

Thanks to Jago's knowledge of the back roads of the city, they managed to avoid the military police. Jago dropped Arda and Ivo at the church with the wire cutters. Arda and Jago tested their cell phones. "OK," said Arda to Jago. "You and Nazar go back to the National Gallery. You'll hear from me soon."

Arda and Ivo went inside the church, opened the secret door to the tunnel, and started running. They ran all the way down the tunnel. All the way to the National Gallery.

Chapter 9

The moment

Arda and Ivo stood at the end of the tunnel. The national collection was there, covered in plastic. *This is what it's all about,* thought Arda looking at all the art work. *We have to save this.* Then she remembered Gora's face as he had told her to go, in the back of the police van. *What about Gora?* she thought. *What will they do to him? What have they done to him already?*

They were breathless. Arda could hear Major Rakov and his men up above them in the National Gallery. They were right there, in the main gallery, near the wall hanging, near the tunnel. Arda could hear them pulling things from the walls, laughing.

"Stay here," Arda said to Ivo silently. Then she went up the stairs, carefully, quietly. She took out her cell phone and rang Jago's number once.

A few seconds later, she could hear Rakov and his men running back down the gallery toward the main door of the National Gallery. Arda had told Jago and Nazar to make a huge noise when she rang, and it was obvious that that was exactly what they were doing. Jago and Nazar were throwing stones, sticks—everything they could find—at the windows and door of the National Gallery. They were shouting loudly, too. Rakov and his men went to the front of the building to find out what was happening. The plan was working, Arda thought.

"Come on!" Arda said to Ivo. Ivo came up the stairs. He held the secret wooden door open as Arda went through it quickly, the wire cutters in her hands. She looked around.

The Banda had pulled most of the wall hangings from the walls. Statues were broken, paintings torn down and lying on the floor. She looked across toward the wall hanging with the handle underneath it. It was still there on the wall, almost the only thing that hadn't been touched. They were just in time!

Just then Arda heard a noise. She looked down the gallery. One of Rakov's men was still there! He had dropped something and was looking for it on the floor. She was standing in the middle of the gallery. Any second now, he would turn around and see her!

She walked quickly back toward Ivo and the secret door. She had almost got back to Ivo when the policeman stood up and ran down the gallery toward Major Rakov and his men. Ivo, who was still holding the heavy door, looked at Arda and said, "Go!"

Arda quickly walked over to the hanging and lifted it. She pulled the handle out and cut the old wires which connected the handle and the wooden door in the wall. It worked! The wooden door suddenly moved back. Ivo had to use all his strength to keep the door open as it pushed against him.

Arda could hear something down the gallery. It was Rakov and his men running back from the front of the building! She took the handle and walked quickly, silently across the gallery. She went quickly through the wooden door as Ivo made a huge effort to keep it open. Once she was on the other side, Ivo let the door move quietly back into place, just as Major Rakov and his men ran back into the room! Arda breathed heavily and smiled with relief. "OK," she said to Ivo. "Let's go."

◇◇◇

"Well done!" smiled Jago.

"You saved the national art collection!" said Nazar, as he kissed Arda on the top of her head.

"With your help," Arda said, trying to smile. It was hard to

~~~~~~~~ art collection was saved, for now at

The others agreed with Jago. It's impo~~
Gora," said Ivo. "You'll get killed if you try it."

Nobody was saying it, but Arda knew they were thinking that Gora might be already dead.

"Join the Jurka, Arda," said Jago. "We need you. This country needs you."

Arda smiled. "What?"

"I mean it," said Jago.

Arda looked at Jago and saw that he really was serious. "No, Jago . . ." said Arda. "I can't. I mean, I'm not a politician . . . I'm an artist. I . . ."

Jago looked at Arda. His voice was gentle. "Arda, you've seen what's happening," he said. "Artists are in fear. The whole country is in fear. This is not going to get better. In fact it will get worse. Unless we do something."

Arda knew that Jago was right. Kalastia was in the power of Zelim Malin. Things were getting worse. She had seen that with her own eyes. How much hope could there be for a country where they were burning books from the library?

're were lists of books that were not allowed on the ⌐ors of every school and university?

"You are Jana Kalev's daughter," Jago went on. "You're a fighter."

Arda looked at the faces of the three young men. She knew that there wasn't much hope for their future with Zelim Malin in power.

But instead she said, "I'm an artist, Jago. I'm not like my mother. I just want to work."

Jago spoke louder now, and waved his hands in the air. "You won't be able to work," he said. "Already, they are destroying your work. They are destroying the work of any artist that they don't like, of any writer that they don't like . . ."

Arda listened. She knew he was speaking sense.

"We need you," said Jago. "Don't you see? There are thousands of Jurka followers here in Kalastia and outside. We are already organizing. We can fight for our country."

"Then there's your name," he continued. "If we can tell people that the daughter of Jana Kalev is fighting with us, it will give people hope. It will help them to fight against these thugs!"

"OK. OK, Jago," she said. "Give me time to think."

Arda knew that Jago was right. She had to join the Jurka in their fight. What about the justice and freedom that her mother had fought her whole life for? What about her own right as an artist to express her ideas? What about other Kalastian artists and writers? Perhaps after all there was something Arda could do as an artist. Maybe this was the moment, the time for her to fight. Maybe it was time to listen to her mother.

Jago looked at her, knowing that she had decided. "We need a month," he said. "In a month it will be Kalastian National Day. The Jurka have something planned—and so do we! We have people who are ready to help us free our country from ... ... inside and outside, Kalastia. In a month

was p

"Good," said Jago. "Let's get to work.

At last Arda had an idea for that large piece of stone that she had in her studio.

Chapter 10

A meeting

Arda walked toward the gate of the Ministry of Art and Culture in the center of the city. She had made an appointment to see the Minister.

"Stop!" one of the guards shouted. He held his gun in front of her.

Arda took a deep breath. "I've come to speak to the Minister," she said. "My name is Arda Kalev. I have an appointment."

The guards hurried around. They looked at her papers. They made telephone calls.

"Why do you want to see the Minister?" one of them asked.

That's between me and the Minister, she wanted to say, but instead she explained, "I am an artist—a sculptor. I would like to make a statue of the Great General for National Day. I have an appointment to talk to the Minister about it."

The guards looked at her, up and down. One of them picked up the telephone again. There was a lot of talking inside the Ministry gate. Finally the guard came out and spoke to Arda.

"You can go in," he said. "You have just twenty minutes. Go through the security door."

Arda went through the security door and followed one of the guards into the Ministry. They walked through the building for a long time and eventually came to some large wooden doors. The guard knocked.

"Enter!"

Arda took a deep breath and walked into the room. As she walked in, she was greeted by a thin man in a gray suit, the Minister. But behind him in the brown

"Miss

Arda tried to smile. "I . . . er," she began.

"Let me introduce the Great General," said the Minister.

Arda stepped forward as the General came toward her. Malin was a well-built, handsome man, as handsome as the pictures of him that were now all over Galata. He wore the brown Banda uniform and tall black leather boots. On the front of his jacket, a large number of gold medals reflected the light from the lamps around the room.

"The General was here with me when you arrived at the gate just now," explained the Minister. "I told him that you were planning a statue of him, and naturally he said that he wanted to talk to you himself."

"Of course," said Arda.

The Minister looked as nervous as Arda. "Well!" he said, opening the door. "I will leave you two together."

Suddenly, Arda and Zelim Malin were alone. Arda's legs were still shaking.

"So, Ms. Kalev, tell me about this statue," said Malin. He didn't move.

Arda cleared her throat. "General, I am a sculptor," she started.

"And your name is Kalev," said Zelim Malin thoughtfully. "Wasn't there a famous politician called Kalev?"

⋯⋯ in Kalastia. Still, Arda

see that he was ⋯⋯ ⋯ statue of himself made by the daughter ⋯ ⋯

Arda reached into her pocket and brought out a photograph.

"I would like to sculpt a figure of you," she went on, trying to make her voice sound more confident than she felt. "A large figure that will stand in the center of Galata. This is a photograph of a small model." She held the photograph out to him.

"Oh?" Malin put his glasses on and looked at the photograph of the model she had made. She could smell the soap that Malin used as he came close to her. She could see he was interested.

"I would like to do it in Kalastian stone, and it will stand 2.5 meters high," Arda added.

"Well!" said Zelim Malin. "That sounds very interesting. I think my followers would be happy with that idea."

"My dream has always been to create something of historic importance," she said.

Malin pushed out his upper body.

Arda could see that the man saw himself as a historical figure already. That was clear from the pictures of him all over the city.

"How long will it take?" he asked. He put his hand across his black hair as he spoke, keeping it neat and tidy.

"About a month," she said. "It will be ready for National Day . . ."

"Of course." Malin was obviously pleased. "It seems like a very good idea. Our National Day would be a good time to show such a statue. It would be perfect. Sit down, Ms. Kalev."

Chapter 11

Kotya helps

school? The man who

she and Gora had been taken? He left his

walked toward her.

She looked at him, still unsure of whether it was him who had told Rakov about the art.

"It wasn't me," he said quietly. "I didn't tell Rakov anything. I promise you. He just guessed there might be something more. It's just the way he is."

"Why should I believe you?" asked Arda.

"Why haven't I arrested you, then?" asked the young man.

She looked at him. He looked serious. She remembered the day that Rakov came back to the National Gallery. Kotya had turned away his face. But perhaps he had turned away because he didn't know how to help them? Perhaps that was why his face was red.

"Well, Gora is in prison," she said.

"I don't know what happened to him," said Kotya. "They took him to the big prison outside of the city. They don't give us any information about prisoners."

"It's hard to believe that someone who went to Galata Art School would be in this military," she said.

"Things are not what they seem," he said. He looked across at his friends. They were looking at him and Arda, laughing. "Listen. Can we talk later?"

She looked at Kotya's white face. She didn't know whether she could trust him, but she had to take a chance. If he could help . . .

Later Arda met Kotya at Zuzu's Café. They sat at a quiet table far away from other people. Kotya was dressed in normal clothes. He was wearing a scarf, which had hidden his face as he walked into the café. *He looks like a young artist,* thought Arda.

"You said that things are not what they seem," she said, taking a drink of her coffee.

Kotya seemed frightened to talk.

"I mean," the young man started, "there are quite a few of us in the military who, well . . ."

". . . who are not followers of Malin?" She spoke very quietly.

Kotya nodded his head. "Believe me, I had to join the military to help my family. Both my parents are old and sick. The medicines, the hospital bills . . . everything is so expensive."

"I see," said Arda. Arda knew that there were not many jobs in Kalastia. Many young people had joined the police or the military just to make money. The city, the whole country, was full of such people.

"I'd really like to paint," Kotya added. "But I can't make enough money from painting." He smiled. "I'm not as good an artist as you."

Arda and Kotya talked more, and by the end of the evening Arda understood that there was a group of military who

were against Zelim Malin. She also knew that Kotya was speaking the truth and that she could trust him.

"We may need your help," she said, "to stop all this." She didn't tell him about the plan yet.

"I want to help," he said.

"This could be very dangerous," said Arda. "Are you sure that you want to do it?"

"What choice do we have?" asked Kotya.

That's right, thought Arda. *What choice did they have?*

Chapter 12

Get ready!

who want to ...
the Jurka. Then there are all the ...
very angry with Malin for killing their leader. They
fight against Malin, too."

They were all at the old church, sitting around Kotya.

"Many of the military would never kill Kalastian people," Kotya went on, "and some of them will actively fight against Zelim Malin and his thugs."

Jago turned away from Kotya. "How can we trust him?" he asked Arda. "If he tells the military about the plan, . . ."

"Jago," said Arda, "don't you see that this may be our best chance? If we can get some of the Banda military involved, we could win this. If not, we might fail."

She didn't say it, but either way they could all be killed.

"And I'm sure that he's telling us the truth," she added.

Jago still didn't smile, but he nodded his head.

"So, we have a month to get ready, before February 25th," Arda said.

"We'll make sure that everyone knows," said Jago. "Don't worry, Arda. We will be ready."

Jago and Kotya started organizing the people in secret. Jago and his friends contacted the large group of Jurka followers both inside and outside the country. People living outside the country were brought in across the mountains, hidden in trucks and farm carts. Some even walked in, across mountain passes, through the cold winter weather. Kotya talked to other men and women in the military who were against Malin. "Arda Kalev, the daughter of Jana Kalev, is involved too," people said in soft voices. Little by little, people committed themselves to the plan. Many had been waiting for years for this moment.

Arda started work on the large piece of white stone in her studio. She worked every day and most nights. She had photos and pictures of Zelim Malin all round her studio and for a month she lived and breathed the man. She tried not to think about how much she hated him. She tried not to think about Gora. Instead, she thought about how much she loved her country. That helped her sculpt the statue, to make it good.

Sometimes at night, though, she dreamed about Gora. She dreamed that she was in the police van again, with him. She dreamed of Gora, telling her to go, his kind eyes smiling at her. Often, she woke up sweating, screaming his name. Why hadn't she stayed with him? Why hadn't she made him come with her? Why didn't she rescue him now?

But during the day, she worked. She had never worked so quickly. She spent hours every day working with the stone, hammering it, shaping it. When she found it hard to work, she thought of Gora in prison. She hoped he was doing all right. She also remembered the gunshots she had heard in the streets. At other times she remembered the young man being beaten for reading a foreign book, or the national art collection that was hidden in the secret tunnel. She reminded herself that there was no other way.

Arda slept for just a few hours every night. She was determined to finish the statue before February 25th. That was National Day and the day that Malin wanted to show it in National Square. It was the perfect occasion, she thought, not only for Zelim Malin, but for everyone.

Chapter 13

Before National Day

"Excellent, in fact, ...
two or three times. He touched his head
pushed out his upper body.

"I think it's ready," said Arda.

"It seems so," said Zelim Malin.

"National Day is just a few days away, Ms. Kalev,"
said Malin.

Zelim Malin turned to walk away.

"I would like to say something on National Day," said
Arda. "About the statue, I mean."

Malin turned around. He looked at her strangely.

"It's not usual," he said. "It's a military event."

"I know," said Arda, smiling her best smile at the general.
"But when the statue of General Ratin was presented in
1880, the sculptor Shota gave a very famous speech about
Kalastian greatness."

Malin looked at Arda and thought for a while. He pushed
out his upper body. "Very well," he said finally. "We will
ask you to say just a few words."

"Thank you," said Arda.

"The words will be written for you by our people," added Malin.

"Of course," said Arda. She tried not to smile.

They arranged for the statue to be taken to National Square by truck, then Malin left.

◇◇◇

When Malin had gone, Arda threw her hammer onto the floor of her studio and went to see Jago at the church. This is almost over, she thought.

"Everything's ready," she said, running into the church. "We'll get these thugs out and celebrate with Gora afterwards!" Then she looked at Jago. His face looked very sad.

"Jago, what's wrong?" she said.

"Sit down, Arda."

"It's Gora, isn't it?" she asked. Her voice shook.

Jago nodded his head slowly and took a deep breath.

"Tell me what happened!" Arda felt weak and sat down. Tears started to roll down her face.

"We heard just an hour or two ago," said Jago. "They killed a lot of prisoners. I found out from someone I know on the inside that Gora's name was on the list."

There was silence as Arda tried to take in the information about her friend. Then she said, "Why? Why? Oh, Gora . . . !"

"Thugs!" said Jago. "We'll . . ." He walked quickly up and down the room, so angry that he couldn't keep still.

"We have to go on now, Jago," said Arda. "Now more than ever!!"

" ...id Iago, as he took out the map of National

...ore both

w...
she needed to b... .

"Thank you for helping us," said Jago ...
ready to go. "And I'm so sorry about Gora. I wish we
have done something."

Arda smiled at Jago. "He hasn't died for nothing, Jago."

Jago nodded sadly.

Arda turned to go. As she got to the door, Jago said, "Arda."

"Yes?" she said.

"Good luck."

Arda breathed deeply. There was no going back.

Chapter 14

The final battle

February 25th was Kalastia's National Day. In the past, under the Jurka, it had been a day for having fun. There were art events and huge meals, where everyone ate Kalastian national food and drank Kalastian wine. It was a day when children and adults danced Kalastian national dances. The Banda, though, had started to use the National Day for their own ends, and over the past few years the day had become more and more of a military event. This year, it was obvious that Zelim Malin intended to use National Day to strengthen his personal power as the new leader of the Banda and of the country.

It was a beautiful, bright sunny day, though it was still very cold. In the distance, the snow-covered mountains outside the city could be clearly seen. Despite the cold weather, National Square was full of people by eleven o'clock in the morning. At twelve o'clock the Banda military marched down the city streets to music. Children waved little Kalastian blue and orange flags as they watched. At one o'clock Arda's statue of Zelim Malin was taken out into the center of National Square. It was covered in a piece of white material. Then Zelim Malin and his guards arrived. One of Malin's soldiers came forward and took the cover off the statue.

"The Great General!" people shouted. A great noise went up, but Arda noticed that it was mainly the Banda military who were making the noise. Most people were silent as they looked at the statue. The soldier spoke a few words about Zelim Malin, talking about what a great man he was. "And now," he finished, "here is the wonderful sculptor who made this statue, Ms. Arda Kalev."

She was wearing a long, thick, into the

her voice wouldn't work. She
remembered his smile when he first showed her the tunnel. She remembered that they had killed him—and others. Finally, she was able to speak. "When I was asked to make a statue of the Great General," she started, using the words that had been written for her by Malin's people, "I was very happy and very proud." She looked across at Zelim Malin, who was smiling. Her voice got stronger now. "For, my dear Kalastian friends," she went on, "it has given us a very good opportunity . . ." She raised her voice now and shouted her own words. "An opportunity to remove Zelim Malin and the hated Banda, and to bring back freedom and justice to Kalastia!"

Arda reached inside her thick coat, quickly brought out a hammer and hit the statue as hard as she could, knocking the head off. A great noise up from the crowd as people realized what was happening. The noise was a mix of fear and happiness. The great stone head of Malin rolled on the ground. Arda immediately ran to the side of the stage and jumped into the crowd. Suddenly people were moving, running in every direction. At one side of the crowd, Kotya's group fired shots into the air. This took the

attention of Zelim Malin's men, so that they didn't know which way to go.

‸‸‸‸ of people moved towards the stage. Malin, ‸‸‸‸ happening, was running away ‸‸‸ men as he ran.

Arda ‸‸‸‸ the blood from her leg. ‸‸‸‸ crowd, and there were children, women, ‸‸‸‸ Kalastians. "Here," said one of Kotya's men, as he gave her a piece of material to put tight round her leg. She had been shot just above the knee and the pain was terrible. The group protected her as the battle really started.

Now Jago arrived in the square with some of the military who were against Zelim Malin. They drove into the square with a large box of guns, and gave them out to the Jurka followers. Some of them started to get the children and their mothers away from the battle. Zelim Malin and his men seemed to have disappeared. A lot of people were shooting at the statue of Malin, throwing stones at it, even kicking it. There was noise and confusion everywhere.

The fighting went on for some time. People were getting hurt or killed all around her, but still the military somehow managed to protect her. Arda looked up at her statue of Zelim Malin. It was almost destroyed now. The head was gone, one arm was missing, and the body was in pieces.

Suddenly she heard a great noise from the Jurka followers. Arda looked around, wondering what had happened. "He's dead," Kotya shouted to Arda. "Zelim Malin is dead!" One of the Jurka had shot Malin as he tried to escape. Now, with Zelim Malin dead, the Banda were losing heart. Little by little, the Jurka were winning.

"Come, Kotya," said Arda. They walked quickly to Jago and the others. She could hardly feel the pain from her leg. "He's dead! Malin is dead!" she cried, holding Jago. Nazar and Ivo came and they all held each other. "We've won!" they cried happily.

"We've won, Arda," said Jago.

"Yes, we've won" said Arda. Then, she thought about Gora, and her face became sad. "But at what cost?" she asked. As she said it, all of the feelings that she'd kept inside for so long came out and she started to cry. She felt the feelings of anger and fear about the national art, the feeling of great sadness at Gora's death, the feeling of great happiness at their final win over the Banda. Jago put his arms around her and she cried for a long time.

Epilogue

Daily News

... justice and freedom ... country. Mr. Amir Kalev will be a member of the committee. He said that he was extremely proud of his daughter, Arda Kalev, who had led the fight against Zelim Malin. "She is obviously her mother's daughter," he said.

Yesterday, Mr. Jago Dudin, the new curator of the National Gallery, took newspaper, TV, and radio journalists to see the national collection of art, which had been hidden in a secret tunnel under the Gallery. Amongst the art was Arda Kalev's famous piece *Light*. He told the story of how he and a small group of people, led by Arda Kalev and Gora Bey, who was killed in the war, managed to save the art. "Malin wanted to destroy

... able to see it."

Arda Kalev herself is back at work in her studio. She is now working on a statue of Gora Bey.

"The real hero," she calls him. Talking about the national art, she said: "I am very happy that *Light* has been brought back, and that all our national art is now back where it should be." When asked if she would now become a politician, Arda laughed. "I am an artist," she said. "I just want to create my art. I just want to work. We have fought, and some of us have died, for the right to do that."

Review: Chapters 1–5

A. Match the characters in the story to their descriptions.

1. _____ Arda Kalev

2. _____ Gora Bey

3. _____ Zelim Malin

4. _____ Jana Kalev

5. _____ Timur Datka

6. _____ Amir Kalev

7. _____ Jago Dudin

a. leader of the Banda, a ruling party in Kalastia

b. Head Librarian at the National Library

c. Arda's father, a retired lawyer

d. a young sculptor

e. a worker at the National Gallery

f. Arda's mother, a famous politician

g. curator of the National Art Gallery

B. Choose the best answer for each question.

1. Why is Arda upset at the beginning of the story?
   a. Her mother has been killed.
   b. Her friend Gora Bey is in trouble.
   c. One of her sculptures has been destroyed.
   d. The National Gallery is going to be destroyed.

2. How does Arda know Gora Bey?
   a. He is her grandfather.
   b. He is an old family friend.
   c. He helps her with her sculptures.
   d. They work together at the National Gallery.

3. Why does the Banda call the art "un-Kalastian"?

    a. The artists are a bad influence on Kalastians.

    b. The artists are all former criminals.

    c. The artists are not actually from Kalastia.

    ~~· ·'' Zelim Malin.~~

    d. Her only concern is pr~~....~~

C. **Read each statement and circle whether it is true (T) or false (F).**

1. Arda lives with her parents.		T / F
2. Arda's mother was also a famous sculptor.		T / F
3. Gora Bey is a member of the Jurka resistance.		T / F
4. The policeman beats the boy for reading a foreign book.		T / F
5. Zelim Malin wants to be known as the "Great General."		T / F
6. The Banda are killing all the artists and writers.		T / F
7. Arda wants to replace the real art with her own art.		T / F
8. There is a tunnel leading from the National Gallery to a church.		T / F
9. Jago is the only person in Kalastia who knows about the tunnel.		T / F
10. Arda and Gora have to move all the art by themselves.		T / F

Review: Chapters 6–10

A. Complete the crossword.

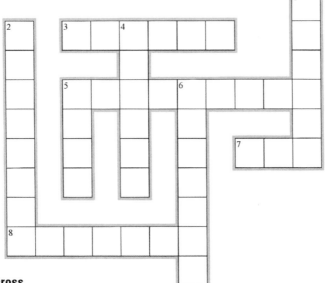

Across

3. Arda realizes one of the Banda guards went to the same _____ as her.
5. Arda and Gora are arrested and their hands are put in _____.
7. Arda escapes from the back of the police _____.
8. The Banda wear large black _____ boots.

Down

1. Major Rakov orders Arda and Gora to be sent to _____.
2. Arda offers to make a statue of Zelim Malin for _____ Day.
4. The tunnel is hidden behind a wall hanging showing a _____ and his horse.
5. Jago says it will give people _____ if Arda joins the Jurka.
6. Jago's brother Ruslan uses wire _____ to free Arda.

B. Choose the best answer for each question.

1. At which point does Arda escape from the van?
   a. at the prison
   b. at the traffic lights

   c. ...
   d. She tells the policeman that Arda has ...

3. How do Jago and Nazar distract Major Rakov and his men at the gallery?
   a. by showing them the art
   b. by making a lot of noise
   c. by calling him on his phone
   d. by attacking him

4. Who does Arda originally make an appointment with?
   a. The Minister of Culture
   b. Zelim Malin
   c. Gora Bey
   d. Major Rakov

5. Why does General Malin agree to the sculpture?
   a. He likes Arda.
   b. He likes Arda's work.
   c. He thinks he's an important man.
   d. He needs a statue for National Day.

Review: Chapters 11–14

A. Complete each sentence with the correct word from the box.

leg	curator	studio
military	hammer	artist

1. Kotya says that the _____ will help Arda to fight the Banda.

2. Kotya is a soldier, but he wants to be a(n) _____.

3. Arda hits the statue of Malin with a(n) _____.

4. Arda is shot in the _____ by the Banda.

5. Jago becomes the new _____ of the National Gallery.

6. Arda is working on a statue of Gora Bey in her _____.

B. Choose the best answer for each question.

1. Which of these qualities does *Light* not stand for?

 a. happiness

 b. bravery

 c. hope

 d. fear

2. At the end of the story, Arda realizes that _____.

 a. she is a politician like her mother

 b. freedom is worth fighting for

 c. she wants to give up her work

 d. Gora died for nothing

3. What is the theme of the book?

 a. People must be free to express themselves.

 b. Making sculptures is dangerous.

 c. If you fight against authority, you will die.

 d. We must listen to our artists.

C. Write the name of the character who said the words.

1. "If I find anything un-Kalastian, both of you will go to prison."

_____

~~~rk We

paruɪɪ..

everything is so expensive."

_____

4. "You are Jana Kalev's daughter. You're a fighter."

_____

5. "That sounds very interesting. I think my followers would be happy with that idea."

_____

Answer Key

Chapters 1–5

A:

1. d; **2.** g; **3.** a; **4.** f; **5.** b; **6.** c; **7.** e

B:

1. c; **2.** b; **3.** a; **4.** c

C:

1. F; **2.** F; **3.** T; **4.** T; **5.** T; **6.** F; **7.** F; **8.** T; **9.** F; **10.** F

Chapters 6–10

A:

Across:

3. school; **5.** handcuffs; **7.** van; **8.** leather

Down:

1. prison; **2.** National; **4.** hunter; **5.** hope; **6.** cutters

B:

1. b; **2.** d; **3.** b; **4.** a; **5.** c

Chapters 11–14

A:

1. military; **2.** artist; **3.** hammer; **4.** leg; **5.** curator; **6.** studio

B:

1. d; **2.** b; **3.** a

C:

1. Major Rakov; **2.** Arda Kalev; **3.** Kotya; **4.** Jago; **5.** Zelim

Background Reading:

Spotlight on . . . *Sculptures*

. . . . has a statue inside it and it is the task of the

. . . . , century, the great Italian artist Michelangelo often sculpted in marble from Carrara in Italy. It took him less than two years to make *The Pieta* (pictured right), now in St. Peter's Basilica in Rome.

Many sculptors try to find new ways and materials to make art. In modern times, sculptors have used glass and car parts, tools and machine parts. One of Spanish artist Pablo Picasso's most famous sculptures, *Bull's Head*, included bicycle parts! Another sculpture by Picasso— known as the *Chicago Picasso* (pictured left)—is made of steel and weighs more than 160 tons. Since the 1960s, materials like plastic have been used as well.

Think About It
1. If you were a sculptor, what material would you use and why?
2. Do you think it requires more skill to be a sculptor or a painter?

Famous Sculptures

Venus de Milo—also known as ***Aphrodite of Milos***—is probably the most famous ancient Greek sculpture. Nobody knows for sure who created it, although it is thought to be the work of a sculptor named Alexandros. In 1820, a farm worker found it buried in the ancient city ruins of Milos, an island in the Aegean Sea. The sculpture's arms and its original base were lost years ago. Today it stands in the Louvre Museum, Paris.

Michelangelo's statue David is one of the most famous works of art of all time. He started sculpting it from a single block of marble in 1501. The sculpture originally stood in front of the main entrance of the Palazzo Vecchio in Florence, but, in 1872, it was moved to a safer location in Florence's Accademia Gallery (a copy now stands in the original location). The statue is huge: David stands five meters tall and weighs about 6,000 kilograms.

The Thinker was first sculpted by Auguste Rodin in 1880–82, and enlarged in 1902. Made of bronze and marble, the sculpture shows a man thinking about a great issue. Rodin wanted the sculpture to represent both intellect and ~~poetry. Its original name was~~

Think About It

1. Which of the three sculptures do you think is the most impressive piece of art?

2. The *Venus de Milo* is famous partly because of its missing arms. Do you know of any other famous works of art that are incomplete or damaged? Why are they famous?

Spotlight on ... *Secret Tunnels*

Through history, tunnels have been built for many different purposes:

Tunnels built for smuggling

In the 18th and 19th centuries, tunnels were often built for smuggling—the illegal movement of goods or people. Almost every village on the southern coast of England has a local story of a smugglers' tunnel. Smugglers brought in goods from boats, to avoid paying taxes on them.

In 2008, the Gaza Strip in the Middle East was blocked and its 1.4 million people were not allowed to trade with the outside world. These tunnels (above) were built to smuggle goods and people to and from Egypt.

Tunnels built between two buildings

In the United Kingdom and other parts of Europe, there are many secret tunnels which run between buildings such as churches, castles, and old houses. Some of these tunnels have been found, while others are still secret. One example is in the east of England. In the university city of Cambridge, an underground passage is said to run from King's College Chapel to the Old Manor House in the village of Grantchester three kilometers away. The tunnel is said to go under the River Cam. But no one has found it yet.

Tunnels built during war

Tunnels are often constructed in times of war. During the Bosnian War between 1992 and 1995, the Sarajevo Tunnel was constructed by the citizens of the city of Sarajevo.

The tunnel was just over 1.5 meters high, and ran

Think About It
1. If it exists, why do you think the Cambridge tunnel might have been built?
2. Can you think of any other reasons why a secret tunnel might be built?

Glossary

battle	(*n.*)	a violent fight between groups of people
bravery	(*n.*)	brave behavior, or the quality of being brave
committee	(*n.*)	a group of people who make decisions or plans for a larger group that they represent
curator	(*n.*)	someone who is in charge of objects or works of art in a museum or gallery
guard(s)	(*n.*)	a special group of people, such as soldiers or police officers, who protect or watch someone or something
hammer	(*n.*)	a tool that has a heavy piece of metal at the end of a handle, and is used to hit or break things
handcuffs	(*n.*)	two metal rings which are joined together and can be locked around someone's wrists
justice	(*n.*)	fairness in the way that people are treated
leather	(*n.*)	animal skin used for making shoes, clothes, bags, and furniture
military	(*n.*)	the armed forces of a country
palace	(*n.*)	a very large impressive house, usually the official home of a king, queen, or president
politician	(*n.*)	a person whose job is in politics, especially a member of the government
release	(*v.*)	When a person is released, they are set free.
sculptor	(*n.*)	an artist who carves or shapes something out of material such as stone or clay
statue	(*n.*)	a large model of a person or an animal, made of stone or metal

thug	(*n.*)	a violent person or criminal
tunnel	(*n.*)	a long underground passage
uniform	(*n.*)	a special set of clothes that people wear to work or school
van	(*n.*)	a vehicle with one row of seats at the front and a